How to Start and Propagate Your Real Estate Farm

How to Start and Propagate Your Real Estate Farm

How to Start and Propagate Your Real Estate Farm

or

The Art of Creating and Maintaining Your Real Estate Database

Pierre Mouchette

How to Start and Propagate Your Real Estate Farm

Copyright © 2016 by Real Property Experts LLC

Published by: Real Property Experts LLC

All rights reserved. No part of this publication may be reproduced or transmitted in any form or by any means, electronic or mechanical, including photocopying, recording, or any information storage and retrieval system, except as permitted under Section 107 or 108 of the 1976 United States Copyright Act, without the prior permission of the Publisher.

ISBN 13: 978-1540896858

ISBN 10: 1540896854

Printed in the USA

This publication is designed to provide accurate and authoritative information with regard to the subject matter covered. It is sold with the understanding that the publisher is not engaged in rendering legal, accounting, or other professional advice. If legal advice or other expert assistance is required, the services of a competent professional person should be sought. (From a *Declaration of Principles* jointly adopted by a Committee of the American Bar Association and a Committee of Publishers and Associations).

Library of Congress Control Number: 2016920562
CreateSpace Independent Publishing Platform, North Charleston, SC

How to Start and Propagate Your Real Estate Farm

This book is dedicated to the many

real estate investors

who seek a better way of understanding

how to make more logical investments.

How to Start and Propagate Your Real Estate Farm

Contents

Section 1	General	- 9 -
1.0	The Real Estate Investor	- 9 -
1.1	Getting Started	- 9 -
1.2	Public Records	- 10 -
1.3	Environmental Issues	- 11 -
1.4	The Investigative Field Trip	- 13 -
1.5	Farming Forms	- 14 -
1.6	Property-Research Spreadsheets	- 14 -
Section 2	Sample Purchase	- 20 -
2.0	Illustration	- 20 -
2.1	The APOD	- 21 -
2.2	Pro Forma Calculations	- 22 -
2.3	Make the Offer	- 22 -
2.4	Accepted Terms	- 23 -
2.5	Performance (Cash Flow and Financial Measures)	- 25 -
2.6	Attorneys	- 26 -
2.7	Interment Period	- 26 -
2.8	Contract Signing	- 29 -
2.9	Ownership	- 29 -
2.10	Buyer's Closing Statement	- 30 -
2.11	Investment Property Sheet	- 30 -
Section 3	Financial Measurements	- 33 -
3.0	Investment Measurements	- 33 -
3.1	Rental Property Evaluation	- 34 -

How to Start and Propagate Your Real Estate Farm

Section 4	The Home Office	- 38 -
4.0	The Home Office	- 38 -
4.1	Operational Expenses	- 39 -
4.2	Virtual Addresses	- 40 -
4.3	Home Set-Up	- 40 -
4.4	Internet	- 41 -
4.5	File Folder	- 42 -
Appendix A ..		- 43 -
Appendix B ..		- 48 -
Appendix C ..		- 53 -
Appendix D ..		- 56 -
Appendix E ..		- 60 -

Preface

The purpose of *How to Start and Propagate Your Real Estate Farm* is to provide the reader with a clear and concise standard from which they can learn to acquire, and operate their info-base.

As you can see, work performed can be accomplished in the user's **home office** using a computer, an Internet connection, and an integrated software program.

The data base obtained can be used in comparing properties within your farm area; purchasing properties; bird dogging; and flipping properties.

Section 1   General

1.0   The Real Estate Investor

The real estate investor always knows about the market, available properties, and the competition. In having all of these facts compiled, the investor can confidently make a good investment. This book outlines the methodology that the professional real estate investor uses.

The following are some relevant apartment and landlord associations:

- BOMA International
- CCIM Institute
- Institute of Real Estate Management (IREM)
- National Association of Residential Property Managers (NARPM)
- National Apartment Association
- National Multi-Housing Council

1.1   Getting Started

Start by determining a location that will be your target area for purchasing properties. This geographical area is where you conduct your search for properties and is referred to as your farm. Becoming an expert in a specific area allows you to be intimately familiar with that location's property values, vacancy rates, comparable sales figures, market rents, and employment trends.

How to Start and Propagate Your Real Estate Farm

Contact the National Association of Realtors, real estate brokers, and real estate investment clubs.[1] Search through the classified advertisements and the Internet, and call commercial real estate companies in your farm area. That is how you start research for your farm database. Two additional national sources that you can use are Loop Net and Costar. Most of the time you will find their offering

> *After you become a seasoned investor, you will set up farms in different counties and in different states. Set up your database accordingly.*

listed under "Multifamily." After entering in the basic information such as state, county, and city, scroll down the page until you find a property that is within your "market" area. After finding a candidate, double click on the underlined text or picture, and a description page will appear. Make a copy of it, and put it in your file.

Now, continue your search. Repeat until you find all of the properties within your farm area.

1.2 Public Records

These are records that are available for the public to look at and review. Public records contain detailed information on each parcel of real estate in every town, city, or county. It is extremely important that you learn how to read these documents because they are the foundation of your farm.[2]

You should bring plenty of change with you, since copies of the public records are not free. As you become familiar with the

---

[1] To find a local investment group, go to the National REIA web page.
[2] These are the records that your attorney, title company, and lender will review if you decide to purchase.

documents you will be able to transcribe most of the information onto the forms that we will discuss in other sections.

A. Real Estate Records

Real estate records consist of documents (title, deeds, mortgages), claims (liens,[3] encumbrances), and other details (property description[4]). These documents protect the interest of real estate owners, the taxing authorities, creditors, and the public. Real estate records are maintained by

- town clerks, city clerks, or county clerks;
- the tax assessor's office; and
- planning and zoning.

B. Recording

This is the act of placing the documents in the public record. The rules for this procedure are outlined in the states' statutes. Generally speaking, this act requires that all written documents that affect real estate, its rights, title, or interest, must be recorded in the town, city, or county where the land is located to serve as public notice.

1.3 Environmental Issues

Recent court decisions have held owners of real property responsible for the physical safety of their tenants and their guest. Environmental issues are health issues. Some issues to be aware of are the following:

---

[3] Taxes are considered an involuntary lien against the property.
[4] A street address is usually enough to find a particular building, but a legal description is a detailed method of describing a parcel of land for documentation that will be accepted in a court of law. Always obtain the legal description in addition to the street address.

How to Start and Propagate Your Real Estate Farm

- Lead Paint: Lead was used as a pigment and drying agent in alkyd oil-based paint. This paint was used on interior and exterior surfaces but particularly on doors, windows, and other woodwork. In 1978 the use of lead was banned. The EPA and the Department of Housing and Urban Development (HUD) issued final regulations regarding lead, known as the Lead-Based Paint Hazard Reduction Act.

- Asbestos: Asbestos is a fire-resistant mineral that was used to cover pipes, ducts, heating and hot water units. Additionally, its fire-resistant properties made it a popular material for use in floor tiles, exterior siding, roofing products, linoleum-flooring materials, joint compounds, wallboard materials, backing, and mastics. In 1978 the use of asbestos was banned. Additional information can be obtained from the EPA.

- Radon: Radon is a naturally occurring, colorless, odorless, tasteless, radioactive gas produced by the decay of other radioactive substances. Fans and thermal stacks pull radon into the building through cracks in the buildings foundation. Radon has been classified as a "class A" human carcinogen.

- Formaldehyde: Formaldehyde is a colorless chemical with a strong odor used in the manufacturer of building materials because of its preservative characteristics. Formaldehyde was listed as a hazardous air pollutant in the Clean Air Act Amendments of 1990. It is listed as a "probable human carcinogen." Formaldehyde may trigger respiratory problems (shortness of breath, wheezing, chest tightness, asthma) as well as eye and skin irritations. Additionally, it is a major contributor to SBS.

- Mold: Mold is a fungus that can be found on any organic material so long as moisture and oxygen are present. Mold causes biodegradation of natural materials, which can be unwanted when it becomes food spoilage or damage to property. Additionally, some molds can cause serious health problems by triggering allergic reactions and asthma attacks. Some molds are known to produce potent toxins or irritants. The EPA has published guidelines for the remediation and cleanup of mold.

- Building-related illness (BRI): This is a clinically diagnosed condition that can be attributed to airborne building contaminants. Symptoms include asthma, hypersensitivity, and some allergies.

- Sick building syndrome (SBS): This is an air quality condition caused by improper ventilation and poor carpeting. Symptoms include fatigue, nausea, dizziness, headache, and sensitivity to odors.

1.4 The Investigative Field Trip

At this point, it is a good time to visit the properties and speak to the residents, superintendent, mailman, property manager, and anyone you can reach to obtain "miscellaneous" information on the subject property. This fact find is called "qualitative due diligence." See the form in Appendix B.

Note: In driving through your farm area, write down the names and addresses of all apartment buildings. When you have returned home, google the addresses to obtain information, which you can then add to your farm base. Since these properties are in your farm area, you should obtain information on the ownership and management (see Appendix D). Although they may not be your competition, they may challenge a prospective tenant by what they have to offer.

1.5 Farming Forms

Complete the following forms providing as much information as possible from your research:

- TOWS Analysis Form (figure 1-1);
- Net Operating Income (figure 1-2); and
- Annual Property-Operating Data-Short Form (figure 1-3).

Create a file folder for each property to contain all obtained forms and information on the property.

1.6 Property-Research Spreadsheets

Now that you have accumulated stacks of information, it is time to disseminate and input the information into the proper forms. In doing so, you will be able to make sense of the facts at a glance.

Unless you have complete control over your property, you're basically a tenant.

Patricia Callahan, President of the American Association of Small Property Owners and a member of the National Advisory Board of PRFA.

Figure 1.1

TOWS Analysis Form

	Subject Property	Competitor		
		1	2	3
Threats				
Opportunities				
Weaknesses				
Strengths				

TOWS Chart

	Date	By	Initial
Updated:			

Figure 1.2

Net Operating Income

Section 1	Operating Revenues	Amount	Percentage	Account
	Gross scheduled income			
	Less vacancy and collections			
	Net rental income			
	Other income:			
	Laundry			
	Cable			
	Vending			
	Other			
	Net miscellaneous income			
	Effective Gross Income			1
Section 2	**Operating Expenses**			
	General Administrative			
	Advertising			
	Auto and Travel			
	Commissions			
	Insurance			
	License and Permits			
	Postage			
	Maintenance			
	Cleaning			
	Landscaping (lawn and snow)			
	Maintenance			
	Pest Control			

How to Start and Propagate Your Real Estate Farm

		Repairs			
		Supplies			
		Management			
		Accounting			
		Liquid Cash			**4**
		Legal			
		Management fee			
		Payroll			**2**
		Other fees			
		Taxes			
		Property Taxes			
		Personal Property			
		Payroll			
		Utilities			
		Electric			
		Fire Alarm			
		Garbage Disposal			
		Gas			
		Oil			
		Sewer			
		Telephone			
		Trash Removal			
		Water			
		Miscellaneous			
		Total Operating Expenses			**3**
		Operating Expense as a % of EGI			
Section 3	**Net Operating Income (NOI)**				

How to Start and Propagate Your Real Estate Farm

The accounts 1–4 are shown only for clarification purposes (if you purchase a property, this is the account to put your funds in).

Account	Account type	
1	Disbursement	Money market #1
2	Payroll	Money market #2
3	Disbursement	Checking #1
4	Cash reserves	Savings (operating budget)
5	Escrow	Money market #3

Figure 1.3

Annual Property-Operating Data (short form)

Item	Description	Value	Percentage
Income	Residential rental income		100%
	Commercial rent		
	Vacancy and credit loss (5%)		
	Other Income		
	Laundry		
	Vending		
	Garage		
	GROSS OPERATING INCOME		**100%**
Expenses	Real estate taxes		
	Insurance		
	Water		
	Electric (general lighting)		
	Fuel (#2 oil)		
	Maintenance and repairs		
	Trash removal		
	Management fee		
	TOTAL OPERATING EXPENSES		%
	NOI		%

How to Start and Propagate Your Real Estate Farm

Section 2   Sample Purchase

2.0   Illustration

Now, after having inputted all of that information and reviewed it, you are now ready to select a possible candidate for purchase. Remember, part of your research process is to determine if the subject property expenses are aligned with other comparable properties. Use your annual property-operating data to do this.

We are using the following listing to illustrate how to fill out the abbreviated APOD and the "Investment Property Fact Sheet." This is typically the amount of information that you will receive in a "property listing."

- Asking price: $2,650,000.00

- Gross $300K, net $201K (NOI = Gross − Net or $300K − $201K = $99K)

- Building size: 22,000 sq. ft. ($120.45/sq. ft.)

- Twenty-five families ($106,000.00 per unit)

- Lot size: Not given

- Type/stories: Four-story, midrise, walk-up

- CAP rate: 0.07 or 7.0 percent

- Tenants pay own heat, newly upgraded

- Electric upgraded to building and apartments; new gas service and gas lines in building.

How to Start and Propagate Your Real Estate Farm

- Windows ten years old; MSC pointing and roof within past seven years

- Assumable $1,500,000.00 mortgage at 5.5 percent interest, thirty-year amortizing, payment = $8,512 month or $102,202 annually

- Cash required: $1,000,000.00

2.1 The APOD

	Annual Property-Operating Data Property Name Address		
Item	**Description**	**Value**	**Percentage**
Income	Rental income	$300,000.00	100%
	Commercial rent		
	Vacancy and credit loss		
	Other income		
	Laundry		
	Vending		
	Garage		
GROSS OPERATING INCOME		$300,000.00	100%
Expenses	Real estate taxes		
	Insurance		
	Water		
	Electric (general lighting)		
	Fuel (#2 Oil)		
	Maintenance and repair		
	Trash removal		
	Management Fee		
TOTAL OPERATING EXPENSES		$99.000.00	33%
	NOI	$201,000.00	67%

How to Start and Propagate Your Real Estate Farm

On this form, you can fill-in the various dollar values and their corresponding percentages. The formula that we use for percentage is as follows: *Expense/GOI x 100 = percentage of the expense.*

So far, everything is looking good! Now let's run our financial measurements. Remember, the following *actual* information was received in the listing.

2.2 Pro Forma Calculations
A. Gross Rent Multiplier

- GRM = Market Value / Gross Schedule Income

- GRM = 2,650,000/300,000 = 8.83 (This should be comparable with other properties in the area.)

B. Gross Scheduled Income

- GSI = Total Rent Payable + Vacant Space at Market Rate

- GSI = $300,000 *(Note: listing did not provide for vacancy factor)*

2.3 Make the Offer

Now that we have found a property that we are interested in, it's time to make an offer. On the Purchase Sales Agreement (PSA), we make an offer to purchase 123 South Main—Mount Vernon, New York. We have computed the offering price as follows:

Seller's Asking Price	$2,650,000.00
Discount (18.0%)	−477,000.00
Our Offering Price	$2,173,000.00
The seller counter offered for:	$2,287,500.00
Original Asking Price:	$2,650,000.00
Accepted purchase savings	$362,500.00

Through negotiating we saved $362,500.00, or 13.68 percent.

> **Purchase reasoning: A drive-by verified that the area is up and coming. It has adjacent public transportation, and the employment market is ongoing and diversified (NYC). The listing take-off sheet gave it a 7.0% CAP rate, and after speaking to the listing agency, there is room for value added features (4,500 sq. ft. for day care, office, etc.). In addition to the foregoing, a $362,500 discount will also allow for appraisal, inspections, testing, and closing costs.**

2.4   Accepted Terms

Here are the terms as accepted:

Purchase price	$2,287,500.00	
Earnest (5%)	114,375.00	
Contracts	300,000.00	
Closing	160,625.00	Total of 24.21% down ($575,000.00)
First mortgage	1,500,000.00	Assumable first mortgage ($1,430,901.31 balloon) currently $8,517.00 monthly
Second mortgage	330,000.00	15 years @ 6.0% interest ($2,532.00 monthly)

How to Start and Propagate Your Real Estate Farm

Worksheet:

Mortgages	Annual P & I		
		Gross Operating Income =	$300,000.00
		Total Operating Expenses NOI=	(99,000.00) $201,000.00
$1,500,000.00	$102,204.00	Annual P and I =	$132,588.00
330,000.00	$30,384.00	**Potential Profit**	**$68,412.00**
$1,800,000.00	$132,588.00		

The land records show that the land is 15 percent of the value, and the improvements are 85 percent. It also shows that the value of the property is $2,450,000.00. (Looks like we are buying right).

Purchase price of $2,287,500.00 – 15 percent = $1,944,375.00. Because of the month, the property was purchased in (January), we have a first-year depreciation of $67,761.47 and thereafter for $70,697.48.

After putting all the numbers together, we find that we have a potential profit of $65,381.248 with a tax liability of $32,938.25.

This is really great because we haven't even implemented our value-added strategies!

2.5 Performance (Cash Flow and Financial Measures)

	Description	Year 1	Year 2	Year 3
	Projected property value	$2,782,500	$2,921,625	$3,067,706
Rental Activity Analysis	Potential rental income	300,000	315,000	330,750
	Less vacancy and credit losses	-15,000	-15,750	-16,538
	Less operating expenses	-99,000	-99,990	-100,990
	NOI	**$186,000**	**$199,260**	**$213,223**
	Less annual debt service	-132,581	-132,581	-132,581
	Cash flow before taxes	**$53,419**	**$66,679**	**$80,642**
Financial Measurements	Debt-coverage ratio (DCR)	1.40	1.50	1.61
	Capitalization rate based on cost	7.83%	8.39%	8.98%
	Gross rent yearly multiplier (GRM)	7.63	9.28	9.28
	Cash-on-cash return (before taxes)	9.29%	11.60%	14.02%

On this form, you can fill in the various dollar values and their corresponding percentages. The formula that we use for percentage is as follows:

Calculation Criteria

- Purchase price = $2,287,500.00
- Property appreciation value increases 5 percent per year
- Rental income based on 5 percent increase per year; vacancy 5 percent per year; operating expenses increased 1 percent per year

2.6   Attorneys

Purchase subject to contracts containing the following conditions and clauses as drawn up by sellers' and buyers' attorneys:

- unit inspection by buyer;
- verification of income and expenses by buyer's accountants;
- verification of leases, lease terms, and rents being paid by buyer;
- verification of mortgage balances, rate term, monthly payment on assumable mortgage, and escrow account balances; and
- appraisal and inspections.

2.7   Interment Period

The following should have been completed in 1.2 above, but for clarity we will repeat it again. *Go to the town hall (assessor's office), and make copies of the field card. After making the copies, go to "Land Records," and check the "Day Book" or "Grantor and Grantee Books" for activity on the subject property. Make copies of all information found. If you have difficulties, you will find the town employees extremely helpful.*

How to Start and Propagate Your Real Estate Farm

Review your information for:

- mortgage information;
- liens; and
- the field card, which will also help you to determine improvement percentage.

improvement =	$2,082,500.00	85%
land =	$367,500.00	15%
total =	$2,450,000.00	100%

Modify "Due Diligence Letter to Property Owner" as it relates to this property, and send it off to the seller. Shortly thereafter, you will start to receive information, which you can input into the appropriate forms and then analyze it.

Due Diligence Letter to Property Owner

Date:

To:

RE:

Gentlemen:

As part of my offer to purchase the above referenced property, I am requesting that the following documentation be delivered to my attorney. I realize that the list is extensive and that some items may not pertain to this property. If so, would you please indicate on your letter of transmittal that the particular requested document does not apply and was not included. Please note that we cannot begin our due diligence without receipt of the complete package.

How to Start and Propagate Your Real Estate Farm

#	Included? Yes	Included? No	Description
1.			All plans and specifications related to any civil, landscape, or site plan for the property
2.			All entitlement documents and correspondence surveys of any nature
3.			Mitigation agreements with any governmental agency and any traffic studies for the site or surrounding properties
4.			Zoning agreements, permits, approvals, contracts, or certificates relating to the development or operation of the property
5.			Phase I or II environmental assessments and geotechnical or soil reports (no matter how old)
6.			Wetland reports, including any mitigation plan, and all correspondence with engineers or governmental agencies in connection with it
7.			Any previous inspection reports and recent appraisals (even if they are old)
8.			All notes and security instruments affecting the property
9.			All rental agreements, applications, leases, service contracts, complete and current rent roll, schedule of tenant deposits and additional fees, management agreements, real estate tax documentation, assessments, insurance policies, and operating statements for the past two years and year to date
10.			Last twelve months of utility bills

11.		Names, addresses, and telephone numbers of vendors or contractors used in relation to the property
12.		A written inventory of all personal property to be conveyed at close of escrow.
13.		Seller's Schedule E.

As time is of the essence, we thank you in advance for expediting the aforementioned to us.

Thanking you in advance,

_____

2.8   Contract Signing

Now that you have signed contracts, your due diligence period has begun. During this time period, you must complete the following:

- Property physical inspection and value-added strategies

- Loan application

- The reason the owner is selling (interview knowledgeable others)

- Request third-party inspection

- Get insurance

2.9   Ownership

Assume the property closed on January 26. Now that you are the property owner, it is time to start getting all paperwork in order.

2.10 Buyer's Closing Statement

Description	Debit	Credit
Purchase price (original basis)	$2,287,500	
Deposit in escrow		$326,875
Title insurance		
Proration of taxes		
Proration of interest		
Proration of rents		
Security deposits		
Hazard insurance		
Survey		
Transfer fee on existing mortgage		
Service fee (origination)		
Attorney fee		
First mortgage (assumable)		1,500,000
Second mortgage		300,000
		87,500
Subtotal		$2,214,375
Due from purchaser		160,625
Total	$2,375,000	$2,375,000

2.11 Investment Property Sheet

Investment Property Fact Sheet			
FILE	10-1	Property:	The Palms
Year	2010	Address:	123 South Avenue
			Mount Vernon, New York

How to Start and Propagate Your Real Estate Farm

Annual Property Expenses					
Management		**Legal / Accounting**		**Taxes**	
Advertising	2,500	Accounting		Real Estate	43,800
Association Fee		Legal	4,500	Personal Property	
Auto & Travel		**Miscellaneous**		Payroll	
Commissions		Cleaning	2,500	Other	6,500
Insurance	5,000	Contract Services		**Utilities**	
On-site Management	4,200	Grounds & Landscape	1,500	Electricity	3,700
Payroll		Maintenance		Gas	
Professional Fees		Make-ready		Fuel oil	6,000
Office Supplies	300	Pest Control	1,200	Water	9,800
		Repairs	5,000	Sewer	
		Supplies		Trash	2,500
				Total Expenses =	**$99,000**

Financing							
Mtg.	Balance	Rate	Remaining years	Annual P&I pmt.	Balloon Amount	Interest	
1	$1,500,000	5.5%	3 years, 6 mo.	$102,144	$1,430,901	$80,958	
2	330,000	6.0%	15 years (new)	$33,416		$18,629	
				$135,560		$99,587	

Potential Financing			
Amount	Term	Rate	Annual P&I payment
$1,430,901.31	30 years	6.0%	$102,947

How to Start and Propagate Your Real Estate Farm

Depreciation Schedule		
Market Value	$2,287,500.00	
Depreciable Improvements	1,944,375.00	85% of market value
Useful Life = 27.5 years	67,761.47	See multiplicand table E21
Annual Depreciation (3.636%)	**$70,697.48**	Year two and up

Taxable Income (First Year)		
Total Return (NOI)	$201,000.00	
Less Depreciation (per year)	-67,761.47	
Less Mortgage Interest	-99,587.83	
Closing Costs, Points	-765.45	
Plus, Interest Earned (checking account)	53.00	
	$32,938.25	**= TAXABLE INCOME**

Section 3 Financial Measurements

3.0 Investment Measurements

The most effective way to measure multifamily investments is to determine the rate of **return on equity** (ROE). **Cash flow, appreciation, principal reduction, and tax advantages** are the four key components to this equation.

Formula: Annual Cash Flow/Equity = Cash Flow ROE

Gross schedule income (GSI)	The annualized sum total of the current rent roll and other income such as laundry, vending machines, etc.
Vacancy allowance and credit loss	The period of time when the unit is not earning and/or bank charges for tenant's insufficient funds. *Use a factor of 5 percent unless the subject property indicates a larger percentage*
Reserves and replacement	All purchases for real property must include a minimum reserve. This reserve is used to cover any unforeseen expenses to the property. Debt service (principal and interest "PI") times a factor of three
Effective gross income (EGI)	The property's annual gross scheduled income less vacancy and credit loss
Appreciation	The amount that the property increases in value over time due to location, property type, rental rates, and other variables. *Use 2.5 percent. You can verify this percentage with your local Realtor*

Principal reduction	The amount the principal is reduced by making monthly loan payments. In the beginning, most of your payment is applied toward interest. As the loan matures, more of the payment is applied toward principal. ROE on Principal Reduction = Principal Reduction/Equity
Tax advantages	The amount that you can deduct against your tax liability

3.1 Rental Property Evaluation

Never take anything that is told to you for granted; everything must be backed up with the proper documentation. Use real, historical income and expenses. Do not rely on another person's calculations; they could be misleading or wrong.

Operating expenses (OE)	These are the operating expenses incurred in having a multifamily home. These expenses include real estate taxes, insurance, water, sewer, common area electric, building heating (if not paid by tenants), repairs, and other associated expenses
Total operating expenses (TOE)	This the sum total of the operating expenses
Net operating income (NOI)	The amount of rental income and other miscellaneous income received in a specific year, less vacancies, credit losses, and operating expenses for that year. NOI = (gross scheduled income [GSI] + other income) − (vacancy/credit losses + operating expenses)

Annual debt service (ADS)	The principal and interest paid on the mortgage for a year
Capitalization rate (cap rate)	This is the formula used to measure the relationship between the income generated by the property and the purchase price. This rate is normally expressed as a percentage. Cap rate = net operating income (NOI)/purchase price
Cash flow	The property's cash inflows less all of its cash outflows during a given period of time. Cash flow = net operating income (NOI) − annual debt service (ADS)
Cash flow after taxes (CFAT)	All of a property's inflows less all of its cash outflows during a given period of time, after tax liabilities
Cash flow before taxes (CFBT)	All of a property's cash inflows less all of its cash outflows during a given period of time, before taxes. CFBT = net operating income (NOI) − annual debt service (ADS) − capital additions + loan proceeds + interest earned
Cash-on-cash return	This is the return on cash invested into the property as a percentage over a year period. This rate is normally expressed as a percentage. Cash-on-cash return = annual cash flow/cash invested
Cash return on investment	This is the amount of cash returned on an investment or the ratio of the remaining cash after debt service to invested capital. The cash ROI is different from NOI and cap rate since the cash ROI is calculated before debt service. Cash ROI = remaining cash after debt service/cash investment

Break-even ratio (BER)	This is an indicator used by lenders to estimate how vulnerable a property is to defaulting on its debt, should the rental income decline (the proportion between your outgo and income). Lenders look for a BER of 85 percent or less. BER = annual debt service (ADS) + operating expenses (OE)/gross operating income (GOI)
Debt coverage ratio (DCR)	This is the ratio between the property's net operating income for the first year and the annual debt service. Simply, above 1.0 means that you have enough net income to make your mortgage payments. If less than 1.0, the property does not generate enough income to pay the mortgage. Lenders look for a DCR of 1.25 or greater. DCR = net operating income (NOI)/annual debt service (ADS)
Depreciation	With income-producing property, you are allowed to write off a portion of the cost basis each year of ownership
Gross operating income (GOI)	The actual income that the property generates
Gross rent multiplier (GRM)	Measures the value of a property when multiplied by the annual gross scheduled income. GRM = market value/gross scheduled income (GSI)
Gross scheduled income (GSI)	This is the annual income of a property if all rentable space were rented and collected
Initial cash investment (ICI)	This is your initial down payment
Loan-to-value ratio (LTV)	This is the ratio between the property's mortgage financing and the property's appraised value or selling price. LTV = mortgage/purchase price

Principal, interest, taxes, insurance (PITI)	These are the total items in your monthly mortgage payment
Reserve and replacement	Money set aside for unexpected expenses
Return on equity (ROE)	This method shows the return you are receiving from your initial cash investment (down payment). The ROE is expressed as a percentage and is calculated for the first year only. ROE = cash flow after taxes (CFAT)/initial cash investment (ICI)

Section 4   The Home Office

4.0   The Home Office

Employees and self-employed individuals are permitted to deduct for a **Home Office** if the office is exclusively used on a regular basis under any of the following conditions:

- The office is used by the taxpayer for administrative or management activities of the taxpayer's trade or business;

- There is no other fixed location of the trade or business where the taxpayer conducts substantial administrative or management activities of the trade or business; and

- If a self-employed taxpayer maintains an office in the home, the expenses are deductible for **AGI**.

Deduction and Limitations for the home office expenses are computed using the following two categories of expense:

- Expenses directly related to the office; and

    o Direct expenses include operating expenses (supplies, etc.) that are used in the business as well as other expenses that relate solely to the office such as painting and decorating just the office.

- Expenses indirectly related to the office;

    o Indirect expenses are the prorated share (based on square foot) of expenses that benefit the entire house or apartment, such as mortgage interest (or rent), real estate taxes, insurance, utilities, and maintenance.

4.1 Operational Expenses

The following operating expenses are limited by the IRS as to how much you can deduct.

- The Home Office deduction is limited to the profit made by the business. You may carry over and take the deduction in future years; and

- Business meals and deductions are only 50% deductible;

- The length of the trip limits travel expenses and the time spent away; and

- Gift deductions are subject to a maximum of $25.00 per individual.

The following operating expenses are not deductible:

- Fines and penalties paid to the government for violations of any law;

- Lobbying expenses or political contributions, except up to $2,000 per year may be deducted to influence "local" legislation (state, county and city);

- Two-thirds of any damages paid for violation of the federal anti-trust laws;

- Real estate examination, or licensing fees;

- Charitable donations by any business other than a "C"-Corporation; and

- Country club, social club, or athletic club dues.

A landlord may never deduct the value of his own time and personal labor working on rental activities.

4.2 Virtual Addresses

Locate a local **Mailbox Rental - Receiving and Forwarding Service Company** and obtain a mailbox from them. Use the box number as a "suite" so that you can receive all of your mail and packages there. This type of service can be found at Mr. Mailbox, Mail Depot, The UPS Store, etc.

Your business address, check, and other stationary should read:

> XXX LLC
> 123 Main Street - Suite 56
> Anywhere, CT 12345

The main reason for not giving out your personal address is that anyone could just walk-up to your front door. If you did have a problem, your home could become a target of anger and retaliation, and your family could be in jeopardy. In addition, your tires could get slashed, your windows broken and yes, the list goes on..........!

4.3 Home Set-Up

Designate a room in your home that you can use exclusively for work. The room should contain the following items at a minimum:

- Four (4) draw legal lateral file cabinet with lock;

- Six (6) foot laminate kitchen counter (can be purchased at Home Depot);

- Three (3) two draw legal file cabinets;

- Large bookcase solid wood 84" H x 36" W x 11 1/2" D with shelves;

- Work Desk (wood 72' x 30" x 30" D);

- Computer and Monitor: at a minimum with Windows 10 Home 64 operating system; Intel Core i7-6700 (2.8 GHz, up to 3.6 GHz, 8 MB cache, 4 cores) processor; NVIDIA GeForce GTX 950M (4 GB GDDR5 dedicated) graphics; 27" diagonal QHD multitouch-enabled LED-backlit (2560 x 1440) display; 16 GB DDR4-2133 SDRAM (2 x 8 GB) memory; 2 DIMM memory slots; 2TB 5400 rpm SATA hard drive; 256 GB PCIe NVMe M.2 SSD secondary hard drive; 3-in-1 memory card reader; 180 W external AC power adapter; 4 USB 3.0 1 headphone/microphone combo; 1 PCIe x 16 expansion slot; Energy Star certified; EPEAT Silver registered; Bang & Olufsen audio; wireless mouse; wireless keyboard.

    - Software: Microsoft Office Professional; Adobe Acrobat Pro; Symantec Norton 360. All the latest version.

- Color Printer;

- DYMO Label Writer 450 Twin Turbo;

- Black and White printer, copying, scanning and fax, or better.

4.4   Internet

Obtain a fast internet connection from your local ISP. Once acquired the following should be connected after the company's modem:

- Wireless Router with VPN - enhanced firewall, encryption and authentication features; and

- 24PT GB smart switch.

4.5 File Folder

Purchase colored legal pressboard classification folders with partitions.

Appendix A

Abbreviations and Formulas

Commonly Used Words and Phrases

Abbreviations and Formulas

ACF	Annual Cash Flow
ADS	Annual Debt Service: all bank loan payments made in one year
ARR	Appreciated Rate of Return (ARR=Amount of Appreciation/Equity)
Basis Point	A basis point is equal to 1/100 of 1%, where 1% equals 100 basis points and .01% equals 1 basis point.
CAP	Capitalization Rate: rate of return on purchase price. buyers look for high CAP rates
CCR-B	Shows remaining cash after all operating expenses and mortgages are paid compared to the initial amount of capital invested to acquire the property. (CCR-B = ACF/Initial Cash Investment)
CF	Cash Flow (CF=PGI-Vacancy-Expenses-Debt Service)
CFBT	Cash Flow Before Taxes (CFBT = NOI – DS)
DCR	Debt Coverage Ratio
DS	Debt Service (PI x 12)
DSCR	Debt- Service Coverage Ratio, or Debt- Coverage Ratio, is the ability to cover the monthly mortgage payment from cash generated by the rental property. (DSCR = NOI/ADS)
GIM	Gross Income Multiplier (GIM = MP/PGI)
GRM	Gross Rent Multiplier is another way to value and compare apartment properties
IRR	The discount rate at which the net present value of all future cash flow is zero
LTV	Loan-to-Value: the maximum loan amount of any acquisition
MAD	Maximum annual debt (MAD = NOI/DSCR)
MP	Market Price
NOI	Net Operating Income is the net cash generated before mortgage payments and taxes. When the NOI is expected to grow, the CAP rate is low.

PGI	Potential Gross Income: the maximum yearly income you would receive if the property were 100% rented and all rents paid in full. It also includes other revenue such as laundry or parking income.
PP	Purchase price (PP = NOI/CAP)
PPF	Price Per Foot (PPF =Sales Price/Rentable Square Footage)
PPU	Price Per Unit (PPU =Sales Price/# nits)
PSA	Purchase and Sales Agreement
ROE	Return-on-Equity is a calculation based on end-of-year performance. Factored into this is the increase in property value and reduction in principal balance. (Cash Flow ROE =Annual Cash Flow/Equity)
ROI	Return on investment: used to measure the performance and evaluate the efficiency of an investment.
TO	Turnover (stable properties have minimal turnover). (_% annual turnover rate = move outs/total # units)
VA	Vacancy Allowance: always use 5% as the default unless the paperwork shows more.

Commonly Used Words and Phrases

Word or Phrase	Meaning
Ad Valorem	An assessment of taxes against a property according to its value
Borrowers	Individuals, revocable trusts, and LLCs
Experience	Borrowers must have current or recent income property ownership.
Full Recourse	The borrowers must sign personally for the loan.
Impounds	The lender will escrow taxes and insurance.
Income	There are three types of income. **Earned (ordinary) income**: derived from the hours you exchange at your job for financial compensation (wages or salaries) **Portfolio or Tax Free**: interest income on bank deposits, dividends, or capital gains. This income group includes tax-free income (not an increase of wealth) such as municipal and state bonds. **Passive or Capital Gain**: Capital gain results from the sale or exchange of assets used in a trade or business or held for investment. Passive income is derived from the ownership of rental property, author's royalties, and income generated from owning patents or license agreements.
Net Worth	The borrowers must have a net worth equal to or greater than the loan amount.
Nonrecourse Debt	This type of financing does not require the borrower to assume personal liability for the loan. If the borrower defaults on the loan, the lender can take ownership of the property in a foreclosure proceeding, but the lender is limited only to the value of the collateral (property).
Post - Close Liquidity	The borrowers must have post-closing cash of at least 5 percent of the loan amount.
Pro Forma	An idea of what the value is.

Rate Caps	The interest rate charge cannot change more than a specified amount during the life of the loan.
Seasoning	A period of one to twelve months. Refinances are generally not considered during the first twelve months.

Appendix B

Qualitative Due Diligence

How to Start and Propagate Your Real Estate Farm
Qualitative Due Diligence

A qualitative analysis is based on your personal opinion rather than measurable data points. The following items are part of your qualitative due diligence.

Seller:
Property Name:
Property Address:

Seller

1.	Owner's name or entity
2.	When was, property acquired?
3.	Why is the property being sold?
4.	What was the purchase price?
5.	How much has the current owner invested in the property since the acquisition date?
6.	Is the seller or lender motivated to sell?
7.	What is the total amount of debt owed on the property?
8.	Which bank(s) is (are) holding the debt?
9.	How long has the property been on the market?
10.	Is the property in default or foreclosure?
11.	What is the absolute lowest price that the seller or lender will accept?
12.	What can the property be purchased for in quick closing?

Tenants

1.	How many tenants receive housing assistance?
2.	Are tenants relatively cooperative and friendly?
3.	Are there any tenant issues (drug sales, nonpayment, gangs, cleanliness, or noise)?
4.	Number of annual leases versus TAW (tenant-at-will) breakdown?
5.	Are tenants historically long-term or short-term?
6.	Are pets allowed?

How to Start and Propagate Your Real Estate Farm

	Location
1.	Is it a commercial or strictly a residential area?
2.	Describe properties adjacent to the subject property.
3.	What type of street is this property on: one-way, dead end, double or single yellow line?
4.	Proximity to schools
5.	Proximity to public transportation
6.	Proximity to hospitals
7.	Aerial maps
8.	Pictures of the property and the surrounding area (present and past)

	Building
1.	Mix of units
2.	Number of buildings
3.	Land size
4.	Number of floors
5.	Framing
6.	Parking
7.	Concern for lead
8.	Elevators
9.	Condition of roof
10.	Condition of air handlers/condensers
11.	Condition of stairwells
12.	Electrical amps and condition of systems (copper or aluminum wiring*)
13.	Electrical breakers or fuses
14.	Individually metered for water and electricity
15.	Power outages because of inadequate electrical systems
16.	Age/condition of hot-water heaters
17.	Foundation
18.	Window conditions
19.	Door conditions
20.	Washers/dryers
21.	Refrigerators
22.	Asbestos
23.	Mold

24.	Insects/rodents/termites
25.	If the property has 9 x 9 tiles, they may have been manufactured with asbestos.
26.	Properties built before 1978 may have lead in the paint.
*	*Some banks will not fund if aluminum wiring is present.*

Miscellaneous

1.	Have there been any insurance claims during the past five years?
2.	Is there an on-site manager and maintenance staff?
3.	Are contractual agreements for trash removal, laundry, and landscaping in place?
4.	Zoning issues (illegal units, illegal use)?
5.	Is parking or storage a separate charge?
6.	Is laundry coin or card operated? Is there a service contract?
7.	Is the owner willing to provide certified copies of income and expenses?
8.	Proof of all rental deposits for the past two months?
9.	One-year operating statement, certified (signed by the owners)
10.	Nearby apartment complexes' vacancy rates, rents, comparable units, and other such information
11.	Major employers in the area?

Feedback

1.	Local police (Obtain the number of call-outs and a crime report for the past five years.)
2.	Postal delivery carrier
3.	Local property managers
4.	Nearby owners (Tour similar properties, and verify the rents and condition of the units.)
5.	Tenants
6.	The property manager
7.	The on-site maintenance crew
8.	Vendors

Hard-Copy Verification	
	Operating statements for the past two years (taxes, insurance, maintenance, electricity, sewer, water, garbage disposal)
	Real estate tax bills for the past three years
	Copies of all current service contracts in force
	Current rent roll (for the past month)
	Copies of all rental-income depository bank statements for the past twelve months
	Current vacancy rate and vacancy rate by month for the past three years
	Summary of capital repairs made by the owner since purchase
	Are there any rental concessions?
	Current year's operating budget
	Copies of any environmental reports
	All utility bills for the past two years
	Copies of any insurance loss claims for the past five years
	Copies of all current leases
	Copies of the most recent rental competition market analysis
	Listing of any pending litigation
	Property survey

Appendix C

Classification of Apartment Buildings

Classification of Apartment Buildings

Class	Description	Pros	Cons
A	Usually $75,000 and up per unit. Less than ten years old. Commands the highest price per unit due to new(er) construction, building materials, and labor costs.	Higher rents and lower maintenance costs. These buildings usually have amenities such as swimming pools and weight rooms.	Highest price per-unit on resale, and lowest initial rate of return. In a down economy, these are the first to empty or have delinquencies. These units offer the least upside potential since there is no additional value to create.
B	Usually between $25,000 to $75,000 per unit. The buildings range between ten and twenty years old and are in relatively good condition. These properties are often located in solid middle-income areas and *are likely the most stable* among the various property classes.	Most of the building deterioration is aesthetic and can be easily repaired. The mechanical and electrical systems are near ready for repair or overhaul.	These buildings represent good value and are prime for creating real value.
C	Usually between $10,000 to $30,000 per unit. The buildings range between twenty to thirty years old and are in good condition. These properties	Cosmetic improvements can do wonders as can the addition of some amenities that the class A and B building have. If you can find a class C in a class B neighborhood, you	Selection of class C apartments must be made carefully due to the influx of high crime in the surrounding area.

How to Start and Propagate Your Real Estate Farm

	are often located in stable neighborhoods and have not suffered from deteriorating conditions in the surrounding area.	have a real winner. Modernizing the individual units with updated appliances and cabinets is an affordable way to add value. Most of these buildings can be submetered. The mechanical and electrical systems are ready or near ready for repair or overhaul.	
D	Usually between $5,000 to $10,000 per unit. The buildings are generally in excess of thirty years in age.	These building are naturals for value-add features as long as capital funds are available. Typical repairs or replacements include roofs, parking lot surfaces, heating and cooling equipment, and boiler equipment. Usually at this age the complete electrical system must be replaced.	Selection of class D apartments must be carefully made since the building area may not warrant added value or upgrading. *NOTE: Some lenders will not lend on buildings with aluminum wiring.*

Appendix D

Competitive Analysis

Competitive Analysis

In running a competitive analysis, you will be able to
- identify gaps in the market;
- develop new products and services;
- uncover market trends; and
- market and sell more effectively.

Identifying Your Competition
The competition can be divided into two groups:
- Direct competitors: businesses that offer products or services that could pass as a similar substitute for yours and that operate in your same geographic area
- Indirect competitors: businesses that offer products or services that are not the same but could satisfy the same customers need or solve the same product or service

Now, having identified the competition, you should only concentrate on the direct competition. Keep the indirect competitors on your watch list since they made become direct competitors at some point in time.

What makes a company competitive?
   A. Housing (products and services)
       a. Analyze the competition's product lines.
- What type of building does it have (garden, town house, low-rise, midrise, high-rise)?
- What is the building classification (A, B, C, D)?
- How old are the buildings? When was it last altered?
- How many stories?
- Are the buildings mixed usage?
- Does it have on-site parking or garage parking?
- Does it have on-site leasing, lobby intercom, a health center, a pool, or health facilities?
- Does it have elevator service?
- Does it have laundry facilities?
- Does it offer heating and cooling? Who pays?
- Does it offer cooking gas?

- b. What is it pricing the product at, and are there discounts?
  - What are the prices for the rental units?
  - Does it offer any incentive programs?
B. Sales
  - a. Does it have multiple locations?
  - b. Who rents out the apartments?
C. Marketing
  - a. Does it have a website?
  - b. Does your competitor use social sharing buttons with each article?
  - c. Does it have a blog?
  - d. What online and offline advertising campaigns is it running?
D. E-mails and newsletters
  - a. Does the competition use newsletter sign-up boxes or any other similar opt-in forms?
  - b. What questions does it use on its forms?
E. Content engagement
  - a. What does your competition do to engage the public?
    - Does it use social media?
    - If so, what does it use (e.g., Twitter, Facebook, Instagram, Snapchat, LinkedIn, YouTube, Pinterest)?
    - Does it categorize content using tags or follow and share buttons?
    - Have you checked out its quantitative items from each platform?
      - Number of fans/followers
      - Posting frequency and consistency
      - Are users leaving comments or sharing its posts?
      - How many shares, repins, and retweets does its posts get?
    - How often does it share on Twitter or Facebook?
    - Does it use paid ads on social media?
    - Is it using a retargeting or a content-discovery tool such as Taboola or Outbrain?

F. SEO
   a. What keyword optimization methods is your competitor using?
      - Page title
      - URL structure
      - Title
      - Header tags
      - Keyword density in the copy itself
      - Image AQLT text tags
      - Use of Internet linking
   b. What other methods of optimization is your competitor using?
      - What keywords is it using?
      - What content of it is shared and linked to?
      - What social media platforms is your target audience using and the most active on?
      - What other sites are linked back to your competitor's site—but not yours?
      - Who is referring traffic to your competitor's site?

Appendix E

Resources

APARTMENT ORGANIZATIONS

The Landlord Protection Agency

1-877-984-3572
http://www.thelpa.com

***

National Association of Independent Landlords

1-800-352-3395
http://www.nail0usa.com

***

Commercial Real Estate Exchange

(512) 537-4404
http://commrex.com

***

National Apartment Association (NAA)

4300 Wilson Blvd., Suite 400
Alexandria, VA 22203
(703) 518-6141
http://www.naahq.org

***

National Association of Real Estate Investor

235 Peachtree NE, Suite 400
Atlanta, Georgia 30303
(877) 545-9975
http://www.narei.com

***

National Real Estate Investor

http://www.nreionline.com

***

National Multi-Housing Council (NMHC)

1850 M Street NW, Suite 540
Washington, DC 20036–5803
(202) 974-2300
http://www.NMHC.org

APARTMENTS

Apartment Rent Search

http://www.apartments.com

***

Apartments for Rent

http://www.forrent.com

***

My New Place

http://www.MyNewPlace.com

COMPARABLE SALES DATA

LoopNet

101 California Street
43rd Floor
San Francisco, CA 94111
(415) 243-4200
www.loopnet.com

***

Costar Research

www.costar.com

***

Commercial Listings

www.CIMLS.com

***

Commrex
Real Capital Analytics

www.rcanalytics.com

***

REI, Inc.

www.reis.com

ENVIRONMENTAL

Environmental Data Resources Corp.

www.edrnet.com

***

ESA and PCA INSPECTION COMPANIES

ATC Associates

www.atcassociates.com

***

Criterium Engineers

www.criterium-commercial.com

***

Terracon

www.terracon.com

***

GENERAL

Constant Contact, Inc.
E-mail Marketing
1-866-876-8464
www.constant contact.com

***

GOVERNMENT

US Bureau of the Census
New York Regional Office
32 Old Slip, 9th Floor
New York, NY, 10005
(212) 584-3402
www.census.gov/regions

***

Bureau of Labor Statistics
www.bls.gov

www.factfinder.census.gov

GOVERNMENT SALES

FDIC Real Estate Sales
http://fdic.gov/buying/owned/index.html

***

IRS Auction
http://www.treasury.gov/auctions/irs/

***

How to Start and Propagate Your Real Estate Farm

**US Marshals Services
Asset Forfeiture Sales**
http://www.justice.gov/marshals

CWS Asset Management and Sales
http://www.cwsmarketing.com/ustd_realestate.htm

Chronos Solutions
http://www.chronossolutions.com/properties/us-marshals-service-properties

Bid4Assets
http://www.bid4assets.com/storefront/?sfid=150
***

USDA Properties for Sale
http://www.resales.usda.gov/

How to Start and Propagate Your Real Estate Farm

www.ingramcontent.com/pod-product-compliance
Lightning Source LLC
Chambersburg PA
CBHW070134210526
45170CB00013B/1012